Sell it Now: The Secret to Selling

on Ebay Guide.

By Tim Swike

Please Read This First

Disclaimer

The advice contained in this material might not be suitable for everyone. The author provided the information only as an opinion by a lay person about an important subject. The author used information from sources believed to be reliable and from his own personal experience, but he neither implies nor intends any guarantee of accuracy. The results you obtain will depend largely on your own efforts and other factors beyond the knowledge and control of the author, publisher and distributors. No particular result or outcome is promised or guaranteed in any way. New theories and practices are constantly being developed in this area.

The author, publisher and distributors never give legal, accounting, medical or any other type of professional advice. The reader must always seek those services from competent professionals that can apply the latest technical information and review their own particular circumstances.

The author, publisher and distributors particularly disclaim any liability, loss, or risk taken by individuals who directly or indirectly act on the information contained herein. All readers must accept full responsibility for their use of this material.

All pictures used in this book are for illustrative purposes only.

Always follow the rules and regulations that Ebay has listed on their website.

Table of Contents

About the Author

Much of the information in this guide is from my years of trial and error. It helped me then and still helps me to this day.

And, it has saved me many dollars over the years.

You can run a successful Ebay business. I'll tell you how.

1. Should I Open an Ebay Store?

Should I open up an Ebay store, or only use auctions to sell my merchandise?

And, if so, what percentage of store items should I list, and what percentage of auctions should I list?

Hint: Knowing this will pretty much determine your survival on Ebay. Thousands of sellers didn't know this in 2006, and went belly up.

<u>Yes</u>, you should open a store.

Why?

Because you only have to pay a final value fee when the item sells, and the listing fees are cheap; around 11 cents if you add a gallery image.

With auctions, you have to keep re-listing the same item every 7-10 days. And, the listing fees add up quick if the item doesn't sell.

Only list your best selling items in the auction format; the ones that will sell every week. Add as many keywords in the title as possible in those auction listings.

For example, my company sells DVDs, so one of our auction listings might be named "Tony Hawk Trick Tips Skateboard Skateboards DVD Video Movie." Get the picture?

If someone types in the exact name of the DVD, "Tony Hawk Trick Tips DVD", then there is a good chance my store listing will show up in the eBay search.

But, if someone types in a general term like "Tony Hawk", it won't show up because there are too many Tony Hawk auction listings.

When that happens, the store listings are not displayed at all. So;

1) **A**uctions are there for stragglers that type in general search terms.

2) **S**tores are for buyers that type in exactly what they want.

The goal is to have 95%-98% of your listing as store items and 5% or less as auction listings. Also, remember to let eBayers know about your eBay store. Add **BOLD** comments to your store listings:

"Please check out our EBay Store for all of your **favorite skateboard DVDs**. We have **over 200 titles** ready to ship right now !!!"

And, now for one of the best reasons to open a store; it gives you more web pages to submit to the search engines!

This is huge!

The web addresses that EBay generates for store items have the complete titles in them, and any other keywords that you may have listed in the title, like "DVD, video, movie, film", etc.

Note: after you list an item on EBay, it takes a few minutes for the web addresses to change from a basic one to a specific one with the title and keywords in it.

After you create an EBay store item, you need to wait a few minutes before you submit it to the search engines.

Now check this out.

EBay and Google have a special relationship. EBay pays Google for higher placement on their search engine!

So, let's say that you have 40 items listed in your EBay store. That gives you 40 different web pages to submit to the search engines each month that can greatly increase traffic to your EBay store.

What is the **Google Base Store Connector**? It is a program that, basically, sends all of your EBay store pages to the Google search engine. Use it at least once EVERY month. This is one of your most powerful tools, so please **keep it our secret!**

You can get it free here:

http://base.google.com/base/storeconnector/index.html

Keep in mind that Google has a new payment system that directly competes with Paypal. So, the eBay and Google partnership could dissolve in the future.

Businesses always have to evolve. Be prepared.

Note: it is useless to send auction pages to the search engines. By the time that they are posted to Google, the auction will have already expired. EBay store items, however, can be listed on Google for months. To sum it all up, Google and EBay are in business together, and that can gives your store items free exposure on Google.com.

I'll explain how to submit your store pages to the other search engines later in this guide.

2. Should I Get My Own Website and Also Use EBay?

Hint: You might know the answer to this one, but you probably don't know why. <u>A website does a hell of a lot more than just sell products</u>.

First, let's state the obvious. <u>Yes</u>, you should have your own website. It gives your customers and prospects a cheaper way to buy items from you 24 hours a day.

The items on your website should be cheaper than the items you have listed on EBay.

Your goal is *not* to rely on EBay, but **to use EBay to get prospects and customers to your website, where there are no EBay fees**.

Remember, EBay cares about their stock price and their quarterly earnings. So, if they need to raise EBay fees in order to makes those numbers look good, they will.

Someday, it may be too expensive for you to sell on EBay. So, you need to be ready to leave if needed.

We use Paypal.com for credit card and check processing, so it is just as fast and easy as EBay. Our web hosting company is readyhosting.com. They are pretty easy to deal with and also inexpensive; maybe $99 a year. Your domain name might be a little extra. <u>Don't</u> ever go for the cheap web hosting companies because they will probably set you up with a very slow website.

To upload and edit your web pages, you will need an FTP program (file transfer protocol), like **Core FTP**. You can find it here:

http://wwwcoreftp.com

There are many other free FTP programs available online.

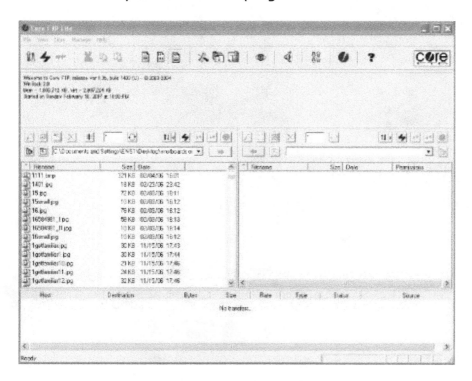

Note: if you don't know how to design a webpage, find one online. I have a graphic designer I use, that does good work for cheap; usually around $200-$300 for a nice looking website. Or, you could look online for html instructions.

Designing a basic website is much easier than you think. But you can still run a successful business without your own website.

Just keep in mind that, you are at eBay's mercy. If they want to raise fees, they will.

Build Your Mailing List

Every time you get an order, you need to save the customer's email address in a text file (.txt) on your computer. You will use this text file to send bulk emails to your customers every time you have a new product or a sale.

List one address per line. Don't use any commas to separate the email addresses.

Your bulk emails will be sent from your web hosting account. Email Readyhosting, or whoever your web hosting company is, and ask them for permission to send 10,000 emails per hour to your customers. If you tried to send 10,000 emails on AOL, or anywhere else for that matter, your account would surely get suspended.

I will go into detail a little later about what bulk email program you need to get.

Just keep in mind, you need to stay connected with your customers in order to keep them coming back to your website.

Note: Readyhosting will ask you to email a sample bulk email. It must meet certain criteria in order not to be considered spam. Just follow these rules:

Put "adv" in the title. This means it's an advertisement.

Put this statement at the end of the bulk email: "If you do not want to receive any more emails from us, please reply to this message and type in "REMOVE ME FROM EMAIL LIST" in the subject line."

Here is an example:

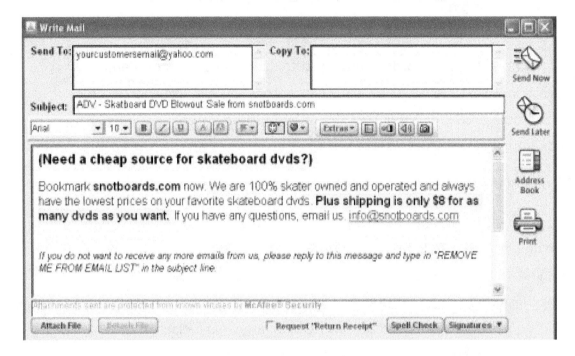

3. How to Email Your List About a New Product.

Your new product just hit the shelves. How do you email 100 people, 1000 people, or even 10,000 people at a time? AOL <u>won't</u> let you!

Hint: You need a simple program that can do all of this. I'll tell you which one to get. This is pretty easy. Go to: <u>http://www.marketing-2000.net/pm.htm</u> and buy **Prospect Mailer**.

It is an easy-to-use bulk email program and the directions are listed on their website. It only takes a few minutes to send out 1000 emails with this program.

You will need to use your Internet Service Provider's mail server to send out all of these emails. This is why you need your own website.

I like Prospect Mailer, because it allows you to copy and paste images directly into your email message. Many bulk emailers on the market can't do that.

Note: I would stay away from companies that sell bulk email services. They are a huge pain to set up. For a few bucks, I can send out emails for you if needed. Let me know?

4. How Do I Calculate eBay Fees Quickly?

"How do I calculate EBay auction fees quickly?

And how about EBay store fees?

How about the fees from a sale on my personal website?

How do I calculate profit quickly if someone wants to buy several different items from me and wants a deal?

Hint: I will show you how to do this fast, so you can email your prospects back quickly with the answers.

You can download the ebay fees calculator here:

http://www.snotboards.com/ebay&paypaypalfees.zip

Notice the example below.

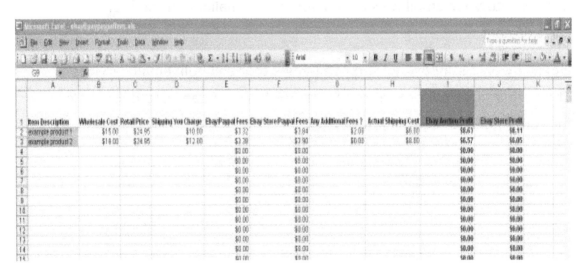

You must have Excel installed on your computer in order to use these programs. If you don't, then you can download Open Office.org from http://www.OpenOffice.org/ for free to handle the spreadsheets.

Note: there are some options in the Excel files that can be changed.

For example, the Paypal fees charged depend on your total volume of sales per month:

If you sell $0 - $3,000 a month in merchandise, then your rate is 2.9% plus $.30 per transaction. That is what your Excel fee calculators are set to.

If you sell more or less than that, then your Paypal rate will be different. We can change the Paypal percentage rate if needed.

Just email me if that is the case.

Also, if you sell in an auction style format, we assume that you will use the 7 day auctions (10 day auctions cost too much money and don't increase sales).

We also assume that you use Paypal for every order.

If you are not using Paypal by now, then you really have no business being on EBay.

Monthly Income	Per Transaction	Transaction Price Example
$0.00 USD - $3,000.00 USD	2.9% + $0.30 USD	You'll pay $3.20 USD on a $100.00 USD transaction.
$3,000.01 USD - $10,000.00 USD	2.5% + $0.30 USD Merchant Rate qualification required	You'll pay $2.80 USD on a $100.00 USD transaction.
$10,000.01 USD - $100,000.00 USD	2.2% + $0.30 USD Merchant Rate qualification required	You'll pay $2.50 USD on a $100.00 USD transaction.
> $100,000.00 USD	1.9% + $0.30 USD Merchant Rate qualification required	You'll pay $2.20 USD on a $100.00 USD transaction.

Remember, these Excel programs will help you to quickly determine what price to sell your items for and what to charge for shipping.

For example, when someone emails us and wants a special deal on 4 different DVDs, we need to put in:

1) the wholesale costs of these 4 videos,

2) the actual UPS shipping cost,

3) the shipping amount we will charge the customer

and then we determine how much profit we want to make on this order.

This can be done in a few seconds, so you can email your prospects back quickly. <u>Always email your customers back as soon as possible</u>. If you have a day job, get a phone with internet access so you can check your email often.

Prospects hate waiting for answers, and will often buy from the first seller that emails them back.

EBay Auction and Store fees are pretty confusing so please check out this page for an explanation:

http://powersellersunite.com/eBayfeechart.php

5. More Sales and Less Profit per Item or .....

Should I go for more sales, and less profit per item, or less sales and more profit per item?

Which way will make me more money in the long run?

Hint: We've done both and will tell you what works.

This one is simple. Ask yourself, "What exactly is eBay?"

eBay is a big garage sale with too many sellers and too much competition.

You need to keep your listing price lower than the competition if you want an item to sell.

It's pretty much as simple as that. Check your competition on every item you sell. Do a search on EBay for a product in your inventory.

Then, ask yourself which seller would you buy from? If it wasn't you, then you have got a problem.

From time to time, you will notice that some items sell like crazy, and then stop moving all of a sudden. This happens all the time, and will probably happen to you, too.

It is usually because there is a new guy on the block selling the exact same item for less. Try to keep these newbies out of the game; sell your stuff <u>cheap</u>. Don't leave any room for someone else to take your sales when you are not looking.

<u>eBay is all about price</u>. Buyers go there for a deal. You could have 100 negative feedbacks, horrible customer service and slow shipping but, if

your product is $1 less than the other guy, you get the sale! Another reason to sell cheaper has to do with the order in which the listings are displayed. It's pretty plain and simple. Cheaper store items show up first.

6. How Should I Submit My Website to Search Engines?

How Should I submit my website to the search engines?

Should I use a paid service for this?

If so, which one?

Don't waste money one any of those search engine services. In my opinion, t hey are worthless. Instead, just use **Submit Express**. Its fast, easy, and free.

Here is the website:

http://www.submitexpress.com/submit.html

Submit Express will ask you for your email address in addition to you website address.

Be sure to enter an email address that you never use, because you will get a ton of junk email in that account.

Submit your eBay store web pages to the search engines every month. Most eBayers don't do this, and that is a HUGE mistake.

Remember that the Google Base Store Connector takes care of your listings on Google (the most popular search engine) and Submit Express will take care of your listings on all of the other search engines - like Yahoo, AOL, Iwon and Jayde.

You also might want to try an international search engine called Global Positioning Submitter. It will submit your website or ebay pages to search engines all over the world. This is perfect for products that can be shipped using global priority mail.

http://www.international-search-engine-submission.com

7. What Should I Send My Customers After the Sale?

What should I email to my customers after I get a sale?

Save an email or text file on your computer with your complete list of products and prices and <u>include your web address</u>. Email this to every one of your customers right after they pay you.

Let your customers know that they will get a deal when they buy from you again. Do this for EVERY order. Here is an example email that we send out.

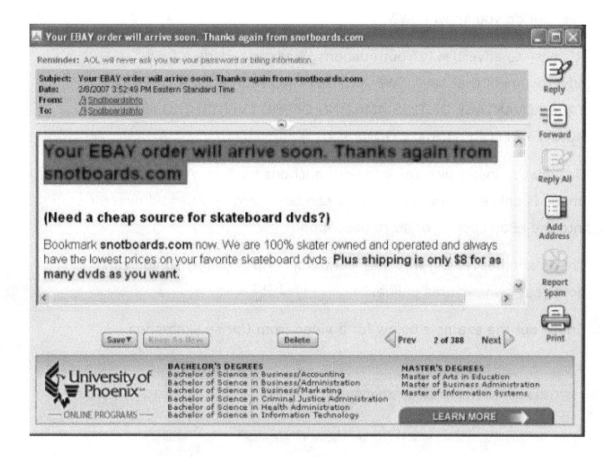

8. Can You Advertise in Your Own Auctions?

Can you advertise in your own auctions?

Yes, but do you know how?

It's easy to advertise in your auctions. You can include a text advertisement that says, "WE ARE GETTING RID OF OUR OVERSTOCK. TAKE ADVANTAGE OF THIS AMAZING OFFER. EVERYTHING MUST GO! HURRY - BEFORE IT'S ALL GONE !!!"

Or, you can insert pictures into your auctions for free. As long as your image is online somewhere, then it can be copied and pasted directly into the eBay auction or store description.

This is another reason why you want your own website; so you can host your own pictures online.

Check out the example below for a video from Uprise skateshop.

We played this DVD in our computer and used a program called SnagIt to capture screenshots. SnagIt lets you capture and edit anything that is on your computer screen. It's a must have. You can find SnagIt here: http://www.techsmith.com/snagit.asp

Why add pictures? Pictures can make a sale.

They really do say it better than 1,000 words and can get your prospect excited about buying your product. At the very least, it will keep the prospect on your auction page longer. So, add pictures that can help sell the product.

Once the pictures are saved on your computer, upload them to your website using **CoreFTP**. Once the pictures are on a webpage, just drag the mouse over them. Then, copy and paste them directly in the eBay auction or store description.

Note: If you advertise a link to your business website in an eBay listing, it will get pulled. If you want to sneak a link on eBay, add it to your "About Me" page. See below.

Favorite Links
Snotboards

Listings

Item	Start	End	Price	Title
7100000609	Feb-06-06	Feb 26 07 22:00:00	316.00	Kevi TRUCKS Blown Out SKATEBOARD DVD VIDEO
7187093083	Feb-03-06	Feb-12-07 20:08:08	320.00	Abec 11 Flashbacks 73mm 88A Longboard Wheels
7105709064	Jul-26-06	Feb 14 07 23:07:46	332.00	Abec 11 Redheads 65mm 78a
7189411593	Sep-25-05	Feb-17-07 14:39:47	67.00	Tampa AM 2005 SKATEBOARD Contest DVD Video
7195504315	Sep-25-05	Feb-17-07 14:52:15	58.00	Thrasher MAGAZINE Beer Helmet skateboard DVD Video
7199007029	Oct-01-05	Feb 23 07 21:29:00	311.00	Element Tricks SKATEBOARD INSTRUCTIONAL DVD VIDEO
7188087878	Oct-01-05	Feb-23-07 21:39:68	312.00	THE FERN RIDING SHOTGUN WITH WESLEY SKATEBOARD DVD

9. Should I Overcharge on Shipping?

Should I overcharge on shipping or will that just get my customers mad.

Hint: Knowing the right choice can save you hundreds of dollars every month. Do you know what it is?

Yes and yes.

Sure, one out of every one hundred customers might get mad, but chances are they aren't going to buy your products anyway.

Also, don't think of it as overcharging. Think of it as re-distributing the retail price into the shipping and handling price. You are actually doing the customer a favor and the smart ones will realize this.

By jacking up the shipping, you can sell your product for less, because the lower the listing price, the lower the fees. And, the lower the fees, the lower the price.

Make sense?

eBay can't get their hands on any of your shipping money. That part of the transaction is 100% yours to keep - at least until Paypal gets their hands on it.

So, as long as your product is the cheapest one on EBay, many customers could care less if you sell a $1 Rolex watch with a $400 shipping charge. It's your competition that might not like what you are doing, but who cares about them?!

Remember, by inflating the shipping and decreasing the listing price, your listings will show up higher in the store searches and attract more customers. And, they will also decrease your EBay fees and save you money.

In our case, we save about $400 a month by doing this!

Remember, "shipping and handling" covers the cost and time it takes to pack up products, as well as the shipping company's charges. The cost for boxes, tape and labels needs to be passed on to the customer. There is nothing unethical about charging a shipping AND a handling fee.

Note: some believe that eBay is trying to force sellers to lower their shipping fees by cancelling auctions with so-called "inflated shipping." They could be doing this, in part, for the exact opposite reason. By forcing sellers to increase their item prices and decrease their shipping charges, eBay can make millions in additional profits.

So, at the very least, I think inflating your shipping by a few bucks is fair and won't upset too many eBayers.

10. Can I Get Shipping Supplies for Free?

Can I get shipping supplies for free?

Also, where can I get cheap boxes?

Hint: We have a secret source where you can buy boxes for a few cents each!

First off, the free stuff. The Unites States Post Office (usps.com), Fedex (fedex.com), and UPS (ups.com) all give out free shipping supplies... boxes, envelopes, labels, forms, etc.

So, if you are going to ship with one of these companies, then go to their website and sign up for a free account. You will need a USPS account and a UPS account to ship on Paypal, so sign up for both of them at the very least.

Once you have an account, you can order all of these supplies for free. **Note: USPS** provides free supplies for priority mail and express mail, not first class mail, parcel post, or media mail. **UPS** and **Fedex** supply free shipping supplies for use with their expedited shipping services, and not their ground services.

If you need inexpensive boxes for parcel post, media mail, first class mail, UPS ground, or Fedex ground, then you may want to try to get your hand on some pre-cycled boxes. These are boxes with defects, like misprints. You can usually get these for dirt cheap.

Here is a good company that sells pre-cycled boxes:

http://gandaprecycling.com

Key	All Length, Width and Height Dimensions are in Inches	Length	Width	Height	Item Description	Test	Available Qty.
RSC J6		6	4 1/4	2 1/2	New plain Kraft	32	2310
RSC		7	6	6	New Plain Kraft	32	2283
RSC		7 1/2	5 1/2	33 3/4	New Plain Kraft	32	1907
RSC Snowboard?		8	8	36	New Plain Kraft	200	117
* FDW= Foreign Double Wall * Stitch or Stitched= Stapled * FSW= Foreign Single Wall							
RSC Wakeboard?		10	10	42	New Plain Kraft	200	132
RSC J13		10 7/8	8	4 3/4	New Plain Kraft	32	2048
RSC		11 1/2	11 1/2	12	Used Prt Kraft	44	32
RSC		12	9	8	New Plain Kraft	32	1036
RSC		12	12	11 1/2	Used Prt	44	25

11. What's With all the Hype About eBay Express?

What's up with all the hype concerning EBay Express?

Should I list there?

Hint: All I can say is that what you don't know CAN hurt you. You need to read this, and I mean now.

I have been studying EBay Express now for quite a while.

Most people say that, as soon as they opt out, they get a nice spike in sales. Some get twice as many sales as soon as they opt out. No-one can really explain it, but opting out of Express somehow increases the promotion of your items online.

If you want my opinion, I say get out of Express right now. I, along with lots of other sellers, noticed an increase in sales after opting out.

Go to your My EBay page, and click on preferences. From there, you can opt in or out of eBay Express if you want to experiment with it.

12. Where, Online, can I Find Out What EBay is REALLY up to?

Where can I look online to find out what eBay is REALLY up to?

Hint: We have a list of some great sites you should be reading every day. You <u>need</u> to know what eBay is up to. This is essential for your survival.

eBay always has some new policy popping up that might slow your sales, and get your auctions cancelled. Or, they have some new technical glitch that you need to know about.

Anyway, stay informed. We recommend the sites below.

The first one is actually the EBay stores' message board. Negative posts often get pulled there, though. So, you should also check out these other sites to read the negative stuff about EBay.

Stay informed:

http://pages.eBay.com/community/boards/index.html
http://powersellersunite.com/
http://www.auctionbytes.com/
http://www.cheatedbyeBay.com/
http://finance.google.com/finance?q=EBAY

13. What should I do about an unpaid item?

What should I do about an unpaid item?

Should I report the buyer as a non-paying bidder?

Hint: No. Do you know why not?

If you are going to sell on EBay, then you are going to get non-paying bidders. It's just a fact.

Usually, it's the buyers with the 0 or 1 feedback rating that you need to watch out for. They are clueless as to how eBay works and can cause you a lot of problems.

We average about one non-paying bidder per day. It's essential to get your fees refunded. Otherwise, you can lose thousands of dollars per year because of these idiots.

So, how do you get your money back? It's simple. Check your items that were purchased 10 days ago. Then, fill out the "**report an unpaid item dispute**" form. Select the option that says, "**we have mutually agreed not to complete the transaction**", and choose "**the buyer did not want the item**" or "**other**" as the reason the payment was not received.

If you try to report the buyer as a "non-paying bidder," he will claim that the payment was already sent and he still wants the item, or not respond at all, making it harder for you to get your refund.

Your only option is to make it easy for the buyer to cancel the transaction without any strikes against his account. The end result is that you get your eBay fees refunded to you much faster.

Here is the unpaid item dispute form.

http://rebulk.eBay.com/ws/eBayISAPI.dll?CreateDispute&guest=1

14. Are There Other Ecommerce Sites That I can Sell on?

Are there other ecommerce sites that I can sell on?

Hint: Yes there are; some are good and some bad, but most of them blow. Only 2 of them can actually get you sales. Do you know what they are?

In my opinion, Yahoo's auction site is worthless. I think Overstock stinks, too. Google's Base website and Google Checkout can get you a sale or two.

Amazon is probably the best alternative right now. It's easy to list on, too. Just find an item you want to sell and click on the "sell a similar item" link.

Just make sure that you know what the fees are. Amazon charges a lot. So, don't plan on making more than a few dollars per sale.

Here are the relevant websites:

http://www.google.com/base

http://amazon.com/gp/seller/sell-your-stuff.html/ref=sv_gw_5/105-7606926-2530044

15. Should I Use Best Offers in My Listings, Even if I Don't Like Dealing With Cheapskates?

Should I use best offers in my listings, even if I don't like dealing with cheapskates?

Hint: Yes!!! Even cheapskates can put money in your pocket. Do you know how?

Note: it is against eBay's policies to offer to sell an item outside of eBay. <u>Always</u> follow eBay's rules.

Best offers put your prospects in contact with you. That's a good thing. That is one step closer to a sale. Often, you can just mark the item down a dollar or two and you get the sale.

Note: once a seller has a prospect's username, he can email the prospect through eBay's mail server, and ask to be emailed back. Once the seller and buyer are off of eBay's email server, then they can make any type of deal they want to. EBay only allows sellers to contact about 10 members per day to prevent this from happening too much.

Here is the address to contact a member on eBay:

http://search.eBay.com/ws/search/AdvSearch?sofocus=bs&sacat=-1&catref=C5&fbd=1&sspagename=h:h:advsearch:US&from=R6&nojspr=y&fswc=1&fss=0&saslop=1&fls=4&floc=1&sargn=-1&saslc=0&salic=1&saatc=1&sadis=200&fpos=46268&sacur=0&

sacqyop=ge&ftrt=1&ftrv=1&saaff=afdefault&fsop=1&fsoo=1&fcl
=3&frpp=50&sofindtype=8&pfid=

Or go to: www.goofbay.com

eBay Related Tools..

Our eBay tools are the most comprehensive on the internet, nowhere else can you view a sellers private feedback, or see a sellers 30 day turnover. If you have any suggestions for our tools range, please contact us and we will endeavour to develop it.

Negative Feedback Checker (Enter eBay User ID)

[Received By] [Left By]

Regular Bidder Checker (Enter eBay Item Number)

[Check]

View Sellers Sold Items & Turnover

[Check]

View Users 30 Day Bid List (Enter User ID)

[Check]

Goofbay Misspelling RSS (Enter Keyword) RSS

[Create]

eBay Fees Calculator

The Advanced eBay Fees Calculator. [Go]

Want a Tool on Goofbay ?

Use the contact form and let us know what you want, we might be able to create it

eBay Shortcuts..

Some useful short cuts to get you to those hard to find eBay pages.

16. What are Some Good Sites to Advertise My Business on?

What are some good sites to advertise my business on?

Hint: We know of two booming websites that you can promote your business on for a few bucks. Do you know what they are?

How would you like to get 400,000 people to see your web address for free? Of course you would.

The first site that I suggest is **Youtube**. It is getting more popular each and every day. Anyway, find someone posting a video on youtube that relates to your products.

Then, send an email to that youtuber and ask him to make a video for you, and at the end of it, include the text "for more products like this, check out our website..." offer him a few bucks for the service. These youtubers can make videos in a few minutes, so give it a try. Or you can buy a video editing program from your local Best Buy, or electronics store.

You can create a .wmv ad or a simple animated gif ad that can be added to any youtube video. Keep in mind, youtube gets a ton of exposure. **Some of those videos get close to a million hits !!!**

The other website you might want to consider getting on is myspace.com. Go there and get a page up (or pay someone a few bucks to do it for you) that describes your business. The goal is to get as many friends in your myspace network as possible to increase your traffic.

Advertising on Google is cheap and easy. You can start at $30 a month for a Google adwords campaign. Basically, your ad will appear at the top of the search page when people type in certain keywords that you chose.

Here is the website:

https://adwords.google.com/select/Login

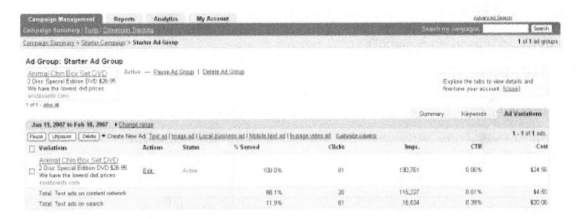

You might also want to pay to have a company drive traffic to your site. Easy Site Hits offers this service for around $20.

Check them out here:

http://www.easysitehits.com/

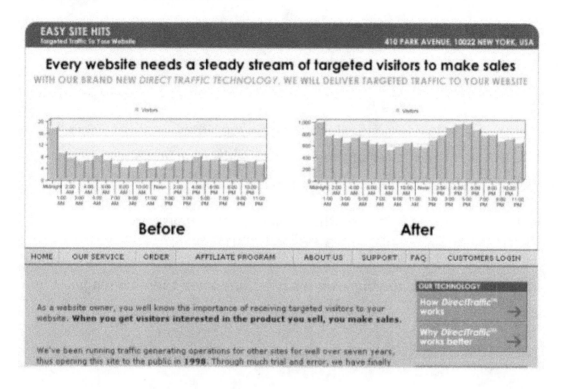

17. Can I Sell on eBay Forever?

Can I sell on EBay forever?

I think it is doubtful.

eBay seems to keep raising its fees every few years, and they keep making questionable decisions, like buying Skype, EBay Express, EBay China, etc. It's only a matter of time before another auction site comes along and offers cheaper fees and more features.

Maybe it will be Google or some other online giant - maybe from China.

Bottom line: get people to your own website, and keep them coming back there.

18. Why do Some Sellers Dislike eBay?

Why do some sellers dislike eBay?

I like to think of eBay as a kind of love-hate relationship.

Here are a few reasons that some sellers give:

- × EBay raises fees every year or every 2 years.

- × EBay took exposure away from eBay stores to force Sellers to list more auctions.

- × EBay put its top sellers out of business, and also many mom and pop stores. Some of the big stores had to pay an additional $10,000 per month in fees.

- × Customer service often isn't aware of any problems.

- × There are always new glitches that will hurt your ability to make money.

- × There are scams and fake auctions, usually from foreign countries that you need to watch out for.

- × Your auctions can get cancelled for no reason. Once they are cancelled, they are gone for good.

- × eBay can do whatever they want; cancel your auctions or suspend your account, and there is little you can do about it. Your appeals may or may not be granted.

- × They make questionable decisions, like starting eBay Express.

× They tell their stockholders that everyone is happy and all is fine at eBay.

× EBay is forcing sellers to lower their shipping rates and increase their auction prices. How does Ebay know what the shipping and handling costs? Do they know the weight of the product you are selling? NO.

Their nicknames include *feeBay* and *greedbay*.

Type in "hate ebay" or "ebay suspension" on Goolgle and you will find plenty of articles from the Ebay haters.

19. Can I Email You if I Have Questions About Selling on eBay?

Can I email you anytime, if I have questions about selling on eBay?

No, my account got suspended, so I am done with Ebay.

20. Do you have Other Tips to Help Me Run a Business?

Do you have any other tips that can help me run a business?

Sure do!

Here are some quick tips to help you run a business.

- ✓ Bookmark every site that helps you run a business, buy supplies, report unpaid auctions, contact members, end listing early, etc.

- ✓ Buy a program called Prospect Finder. You can enter keywords, and it will find targeted email addresses online. Get it here: http://www.marketing-2000.net/pf.htm

- ✓ Bookmark this webpage: www.goofbay.com It will help you cancel auctions, file claims and look up users.

- ✓ Put up a link section on your business website, trade links with as many websites as possible. Check your traffic every week.

- ✓ Save all of your common email responses in a text file. Don't waste time typing the same stuff over and over again.

- ✓ If you are lucky enough to be the first selller on eBay to offer a unique product, do not put the manufacturer's name in the listing or description. Do not let your competition know how to compete with you on eBay.

✓ Never give out your sources for products.

✓ If possible, make up a fake name for the product.

✓ When you are on the PayPal "payments received" screen, copy and paste your orders into an Excel© file. Then, click on the details links.

This brings up the PayPal payment screen to open up your orders.

Paste the buyers email somewhere into the Excel© file, too.

If you get a question about an order that took place months ago, you can pull it up quickly just by knowing their email address. You can also add notes to the Excel© file.

Type the sale price in one column and the Paypal fees in another column.

You can then add them up in Excel© to check total sales and fees for tax time.

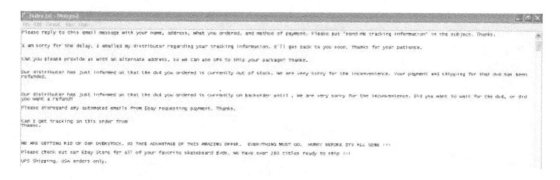

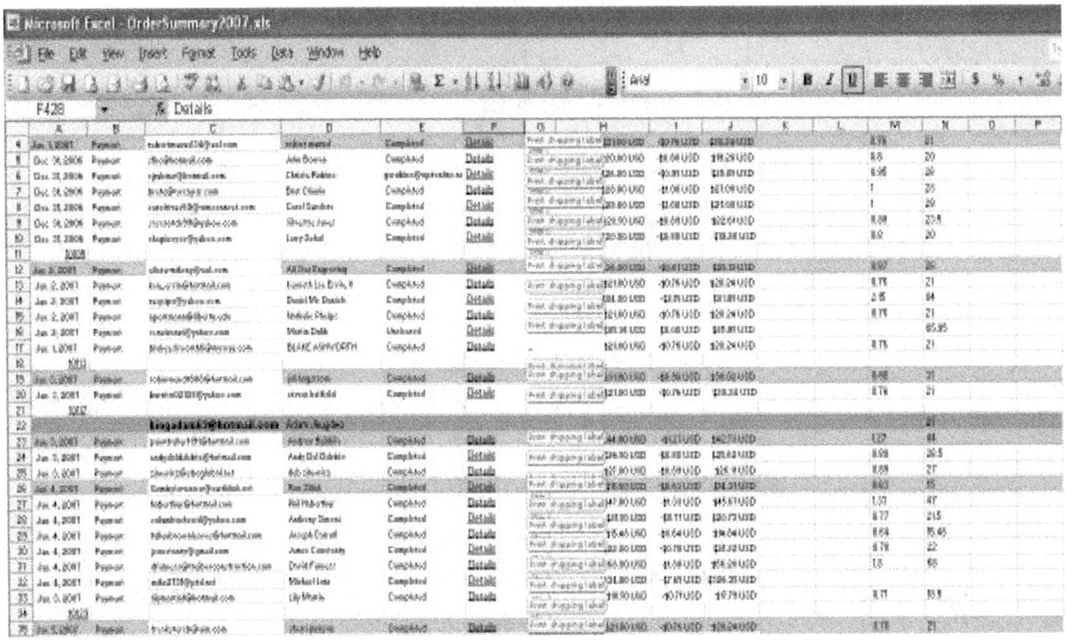
Microsoft Excel - OrderSummary2007.xls
File Edit View Insert Format Tools Data Window Help
Arial
10
F428
Details

21. The Top Ten Mistakes Sellers Make in Their

Titles and Descriptions?

What are the top ten mistakes sellers make in their titles and descriptions?

1) Wrong keywords.

The title must have the exact keywords that buyers will type in when doing a search. For each product you sell, ask yourself what would you type in on eBay to find this product?

Include any extra relevant keywords.

Since we sell skateboard DVDs online, we try to include these words in every title: skateboard, skateboards, DVD, video, movie, film and skateboarding.

Also, do not use any extra punctuation like commas. Keep each word separate. Here is a common example for a DVD about the skateboard legend, Chrisitan Hosoi. The auction's title should be, "Rising Son The Legend of Skateboarder Christian Hosoi DVD".

If you just put "Rising Son dvd" in the title, you are going to miss potential customers looking for Christian Hosoi products.

2) Not telling the customer why they should buy your product.

In other words; WHAT'S IN IT FOR THE CUSTOMER if they buy this product? Will it help him to MAKE MONEY, LOSE WEIGHT, BE SUCCESSFUL etc?

3) Boring Auctions.

If you are not *excited* by the Auction, WHY SHOULD THE CUSTOMER BE? Is this the greatest product in the world, or not?

4) Not Making a Quick Impact.

HIT THEM IN THE HEAD with just a few words!. For example, "**LOSE 10 POUNDS IN 30 DAYS!**" They should want to buy your product without even reading the description.

5) No Call to Action.

Use a *CALL TO ACTION*. Tell the customer what he needs to do! "*DON'T DELAY, BUY THIS PRODUCT TODAY BEFORE THEY ARE ALL GONE!*"

6) Not Solving a Problem.

What **problem** are you solving for the buyer if they buy your product? Even a paper clip organizes your stacks of paper. Every good product solves a problem. What does your product fix for them?

7) Selling the Same Product Everyone Else is Selling.

Make your product UNIQUE, NEW and IMPROVED. Even if it's the same, make it sound different or better in some way.

8) Wasting Space on Useless Information.

You only have a few words to get the sale, so don't waste time talking about your hobbies. <u>No-one cares</u>. If any text doesn't lead to a sale, get rid of it.

9) Not Staying Connected with Your Customers.

If you only use email as a contact, check it often. Tell your customers to please email you if ever they have any questions. Appear to be well-connected with your customers. Make them feel that you are easy to get to.

10) Fake Claims.

Don't make false claims or ones that appear fake. Prospects are not stupid. If your customers think your auctions are phony, then they won't trust you. This is why you didn't buy one of those, "Stay at Home and Make $100,000" books.

22. Any More Tips?

Yes, give your customers something for free. Find an ebook online that relates to your products. Usually you can buy these for $2 with resale rights. Then, when you get an order, email it to your customers as a gift. Check out this site: http://www.2buckebooks.com

23. Downloading the Ebook

You can download the ebook version here.

http://www.snotboards.com/sellitnow.zip

This version will make it easier for you to download the links listed in this book.

- 57 -